What Am I?

by Jim Maddux

photographs by Wayne Calabrese

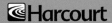

Orlando   Boston   Dallas   Chicago   San Diego

www.harcourtschool.com

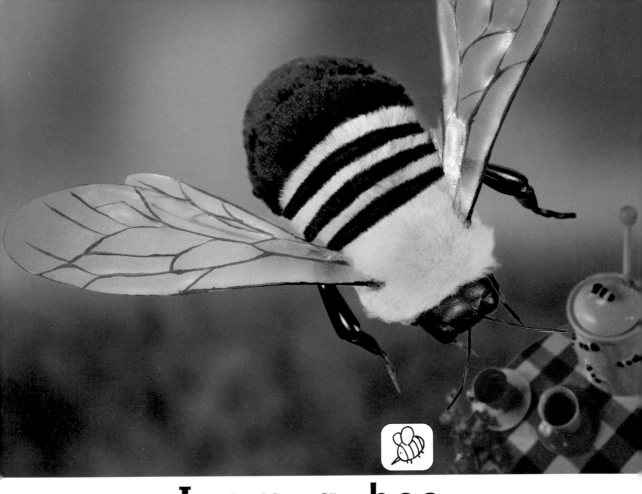

I am a bee.

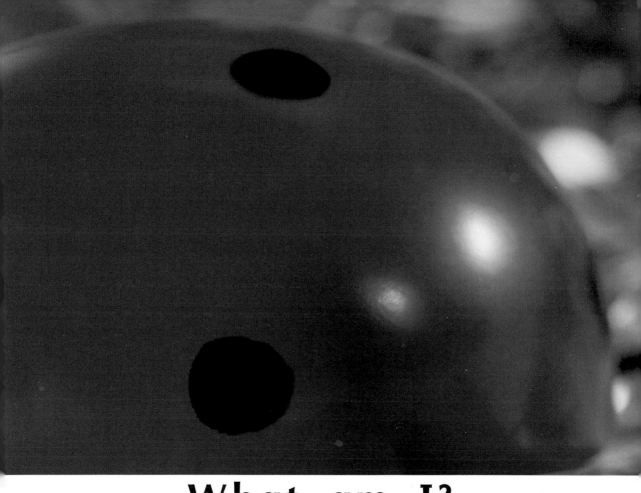

What am I?

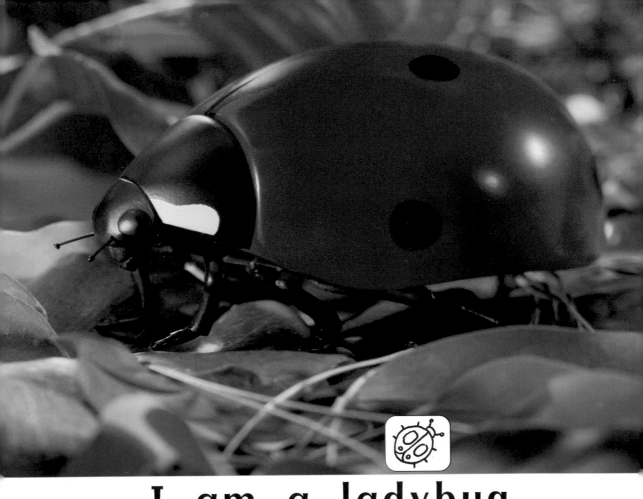

I am a ladybug.

4

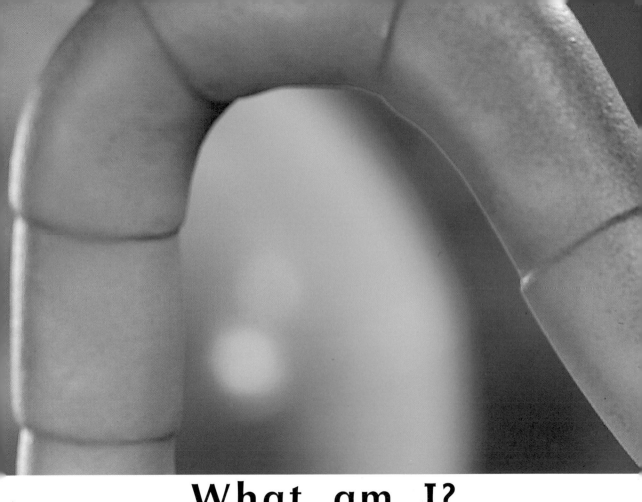

What am I?

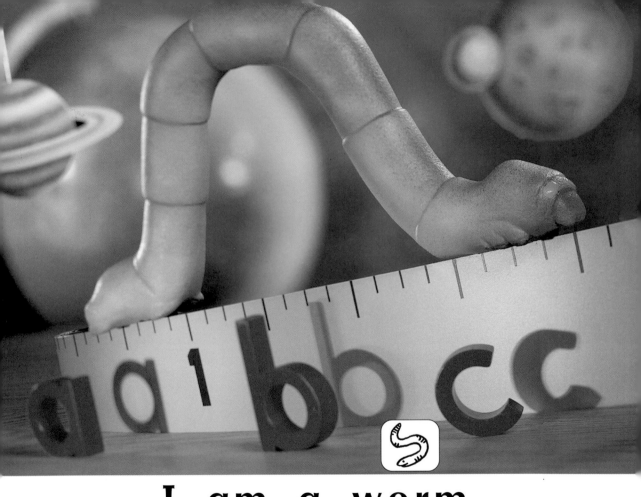

I am a worm.

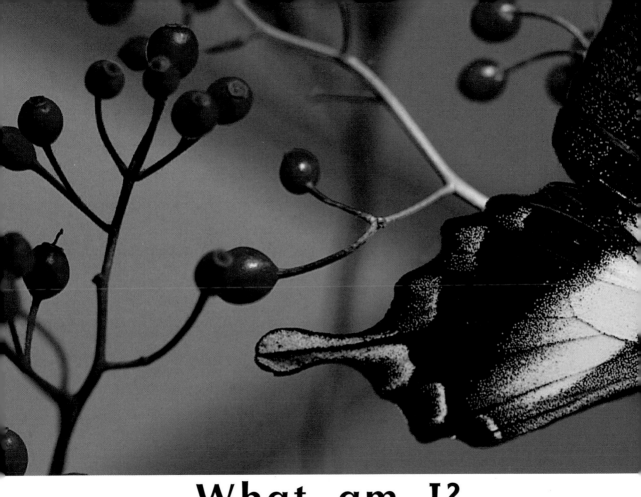

What am I?

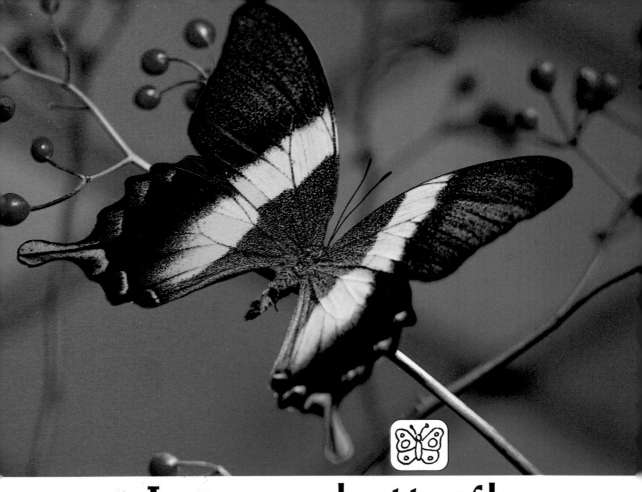

I am a butterfly.